CONTENTS

FORWARD	1
Where Do I Belong?	2
All These Questions...	4
Got Answers?	5
Let's Cruise!	6
Flying Out	7
The Waiting Place	8
The COURT Yard	9
...And the New Judge is...	11
What Happens to Repeat Evil Doers?	13
What Is Perfect Justice?	14
...But I Have a Thousand Questions	15
Return to the Wreck Site	17
Deadly Details	18
Everything Changed!	19
Don't Talk About It	22
Prove It to Me	23
Tell Everybody!	25
Was It a Dream?	26
ABOUT DEATH	28
What is Death Like?	29

What Happens When We Die?	30
What Happens AFTER We Die?	31
What Happens to Our Consciousness When We Pass On?	32
Where Do We Go Right After Death?	33
Does Everyone Go to Heaven?	34
Heaven, Can We Choose to Go NOW?	35
Is there a Good Place and a Bad Place Where People Go for Eternity?	36
What Makes Those Places Good and Bad?	37
...Returned...	38
Why Didn't Somebody Tell Me?	39
ABOUT THE AFTERLIFE	40
Is There an Afterlife for Everyone, or Just Some People?	42
Do We Have a Physical Body in the Afterlife?	43
What Effect Do Expectations Have?	44
Do We Retain Our Identity and Individuality?	45
Is the Afterlife a Place, a State of Mind, or Something Else Entirely?	46
Is the Afterlife a Permanent State, or Can We Move on From It?	47
Can We Find Peace in the Afterlife?	48
Is there a Way to Communicate with the Afterlife?	49
Can We Communicate with the Living from the Afterlife?	50
Do We Have a Choice Whether to Stay?	52
Can We Choose Our Own Destiny?	53
Is There a Way to Avoid the Afterlife Altogether?	54
Can We Choose to Return to Our Body After Experiencing the Afterlife?	55
How Do NDE's Relate to the Afterlife?	56

Can We Revisit Past Lives from the Afterlife?	57
Do We Experience Pain in the Afterlife?	58
Can We Be Reborn?	59
Can We Experience Different Dimensions?	60
ABOUT LOVE	61
How Can We Have a Personal Relationship with God?	62
Help if You Can	63
Looking for Love	64
Does My DECEASED Loved One MISS ME?	65
Crying for Ourselves!	67
FREEDOM FROM FEAR	68
Living Without FEAR?	69
Has Anyone Been Hit in Heaven?	71
ABOUT PRAYER	72
What Is the Best Kind of Prayer?	73
Do We HAVE TO Kneel When Praying?	74
RANDOM QUESTIONS AND ANSWERS	75
Why Did God Create Humans?	76
Why Give Humans Free Will?	77
What Are We Supposed to Be Doing Here?	78
What IS the Meaning of Life?	79
It Makes NO Sense to Hate!	80
Is There a Limit to God's Forgiveness?	81
How Can We Make Amends for Past Mistakes?	82
How Can We Best Serve Others?	83
Why Do Some People Seem to Have More Blessings Than Others?	84
Why Do Bad Things Happen to Good People?	85

How Can We Trust God's Plan When Things Are Going Wrong??	86
What About a Few, Mostly LITTLE LIES?	87
How Can We Find True Happiness?	88
How Can We Live a Life Free from Worry and Anxiety and Find Peace in a Chaotic World?	89
What is the Key to a Successful Marriage or Relationship?	90
How Can We Discern God's Will for Our Lives?	91
What is the Best Way to Spread the Message of God's Love?	92
List of UNKNOWNS	93
Do Our Pets Have an Afterlife, and Can We Be Reunited with Them?	94
Do We Meet Our Loved Ones (Who Have Passed Away) in the Afterlife?	95
Is There a Hierarchy or Social Order in the Afterlife?	96
Can We Change Our Appearance or Form in the Afterlife?	97
Why Did Jesus Allow Himself to be Crucified?	98
How Can We Discern Right from Wrong?	99
One Knew Him at 30 Years Old, One at 70...Which Will I See?	100
What is the Purpose of Suffering?	101
What is the Role of Faith in Our Lives?	102
How Can We Cultivate a Life of Gratitude?	103
What Is the Significance of Miracles?	104
How Can We Overcome Addiction and Temptation?	105
How Can We Heal from Emotional and Spiritual Wounds?	106
How Can We Reconcile Science and Religion?	107
Do You Sleep in Heaven?	108
Is There Sex in Heaven?	109

Do We Eat in Heaven?	110
Who Would Have a Better Understanding	111
Get Ye to Heaven	112
Wasted Time	113
THAT is hell.	115
THE END	116

FORWARD

This is the true story of a kid, searching for his place in the world, that asked for the impossible and GOT IT in a very unexpected way. When asking for the impossible the answer is usually a complete surprise and equally mind-boggling, like it was in the case of his near-death experience. He got long-sought answers to his questions which, by their simplicity, are especially rare evidence of having experienced this as reported.

The following pages include many of the specific questions answered during that life-altering near-death experience (NDE) as well as random questions from the public. Many of the answers received were unexpectedly transformational, even challenging long-held beliefs.

These pages were not written in order to point an accusing finger at anyone for anything. It was written for passing along information. Information that apparently is hard to come by. (Few people have NDE's and even fewer talk about them.) Information a certain kid felt was crucial for living a life that he could feel in the end was worth living.

WHERE DO I BELONG?

Bobby was a rambunctious child with a seemingly insatiable appetite for knowledge. He was always asking questions about the world around him, from the mysteries of the universe to the workings of everyday life. This inquisitive nature left Bobby feeling like he was missing something. He had been raised with stories from the Bible, but he found that those explanations only scratched the surface of the deeper questions he had about life and death.

As Bobby grew older his questions only became more difficult to answer. He wondered why we are here, what our purpose is and what it means to live a good life. He saw that many people around him seemed content to live in relative comfort and not question the meaning of their existence. But for Bobby this was not enough. He had a deep-seated need to understand his place in the world.

Eventually, it was decided that the only way to truly understand life was to experience it to the fullest. He had traveled to different parts of the world. He made new friends and learned valuable life lessons along the way.

Bobby still found himself searching for answers. He had hoped that by experiencing different aspects of life he would gain a deeper understanding of its' meaning. But instead, he found that the more he learned, the more questions he had. He felt like he was searching for... something.

So, Bobby pleaded towards the heavens, hoping that the answers to his questions would be revealed to him. He believed that what he sought could only come from a higher power, and he was willing to do anything to find it.

In the end Bobby's quest for understanding led him down

a path of self-discovery that few people ever experience. His curiosity and unshakeable faith helped him all through his life. He found the answers he was looking for and then some.

ALL THESE QUESTIONS...

As Bobby matured, he became increasingly fascinated by the concept of the afterlife. He found himself pondering what happens to us when we die, where we go, and if there is a Heaven that everyone goes to. His mind was filled with questions such as whether we can choose to leave this world for a better place, and whether there are separate good and bad places where we may spend eternity.

Bobby's curiosity went beyond just the location and quality of the afterlife, however. He also wondered about the presence of various people, such as Jesus, Jehovah, Allah, Buddha and Hendrix and how they fit into the picture. He questioned how eternity can exist, and whether anyone has ever seen those supposed places and returned to tell the tale.

In his search for answers, Bobby started questioning common religious practices. He wondered whether kneeling during prayer was necessary and if closing his eyes during prayer was important. He had heard that God may not listen to such "unrespectful" prayers, which made him wonder whether he was communicating effectively with God.

All of these questions eventually led Bobby to a breaking point. He felt an overwhelming desire to know the truth, and says he vividly remembers the day when he cried out to the heavens, demanding answers... as if he COULD demand answers...

GOT ANSWERS?

Once again, but with FEELING, Bobby said he would do ANYTHING to have the answers he sought. Only this time he hears, without hesitation, "Even if it means being called crazy?" Bobby replied, "Anything!". "You can have those answers, but it's going to cost you. It will be something that will greatly affect you personally and detract from what you will want to do with your life later." He just had to know, so he willingly agreed.

Bobby was desperate to hear the answers to his questions about the afterlife and was willing to do anything to get them. Despite his willingness and possible "agreement"... he received no answers. Bobby waited patiently again and again, pleading as hard as he could, but nothing happened. He started to question whether he had actually made a deal with "those" voices, the same ones that "crazy" people blame for their misdeeds.

He continued searching, and his list of questions kept getting longer, and he became increasingly frustrated. Time passed, but there were still no great changes or answers to his questions forthcoming.

LET'S CRUISE!

Bobby had been focused on living his life for the next couple of years from the day he made the deal for answers. Now 17, he was unsure of what to do next, like many others his age. However, a life-altering event occurred when a drunk driver pulled in front of Bobby's car while he was cruising with a friend. There was only about a second to react before the impact occurred. The car skidded for what seemed like an eternity before colliding with a pickup truck that had failed to yield the right of way. There were no airbags then, so all they could do was hope to survive. This changed EVERYTHING for Bobby.

FLYING OUT

The world went dark. He found himself disoriented, rushing forward at an incredible speed, with no airplane or visible walls or floor around him! In just a few seconds, he left the universe behind, and was left wondering where he was going. Using the estimated size of the universe for the calculation, Bobby estimated that he traveled a distance of 10.29 trillion miles in just five seconds, which would put him at a distance of 247 trillion miles from Earth in two minutes. The speed he traveled at was loosely calculated at 7.41 quadrillion miles per hour, a truly astonishing speed!!

THE WAITING PLACE

One comment that Bob repeatedly hears when discussing this topic is that this was a dream and the people who have these dreams simply dream what they learned in their childhood. That is SO not the case here!

When Bobby stopped flying, he was in a strange and empty place, feeling confused and waiting for something... ANYTHING to happen.

There is no light and no one around. He can't focus enough to think of something to do. Looking into the infinite blackness, he realizes that "time"... IS MISSING! He starts wondering, "I must be dead." He holds on to his tremendous faith and the belief that Jesus will be there, as promised, even in death. "Well, if I'm dead, then where is Jesus? He said He would be there when we die and I believed it...and I still do, so... Just as he is about to lose his marbles, something happens...

THE COURT YARD

Suddenly he found himself in a new place, standing, looking down at his feet (not a ghost tail... or clouds) as he felt an overwhelming sense of relief... and love. The room was very brightly lit. Bobby wondered where the light was coming from. He couldn't help but think of Jesus, who is often depicted with light surrounding Him.

Bobby wants to look up and see if it is Jesus. ...Can he? DARE he?? His knees buckle. Here comes the floor. Now on his knees, after fighting it all the way down, he feels absolutely unworthy to be in this place, he falls further, until he's face down on the floor. But THAT is not enough either and he turns his cheek to the floor! But Bobby had waited for this moment for most of his (sentient) life and NEEDED to see. What he sees is... his life FLASH before his eyes!

For just an INSTANT there is a very odd parade of memories of everything Bobby did in his lifetime. This life "review" is tremendously thorough. Every act, every second of every waking moment of what WAS your life will be INSPECTED in exquisite detail, not just casually viewed. Thoughts count too... that doesn't seem fair, but you would think it must be, given where you are.

One other thing that didn't seem fair. The second you begin to explain WHY an incident that looks especially bad for you is no big deal by saying, "Yeah, but...", the conversation will go on without you. That's not good.

Confused and struggling, using every ounce of strength he could muster, he manages to slowly raise his head. The light is too bright. ...It feels like it's made of... LOVE! Figure that out! It doesn't hurt the eyes. He's straining, thinking, "I've got to see...". It's now or never... He sees through the light... the face of... Jesus! He looks different than any portrait, Bobby said. Bobby celebrates saying, "I knew it was true! I knew it was TRUE!!". Now maybe he could get the answers he's been looking for.

...AND THE NEW JUDGE IS...

Things in Heaven are Simple and Perfect. Do you recognize the phrase, "Judge not and you shall not be judged."?

At a crime scene, what evidence can usually give the police an open and shut case? Video. Who would have the best copy of the video of your life? That is who should do the judging, in a perfect world.

It's been said that God wouldn't send people to hell. Surprisingly, the trip to the afterlife CLEARLY showed that to be correct. Who could have known...

It will be done with a newly acquired knowledge of Perfect Justice. It is the most perfect and simple method imaginable. We choose every act we do, and by doing so we create what we will live with in the next life, good or bad.

It always seemed that God must be everywhere, watching everyone, every second, somehow, and THAT would be used as evidence against us at the final judgement. Wrong AGAIN. This came as a HUGE surprise... At the life review, YOU ARE THE JUDGE! There's one rule. No free pass, even when you are the judge.

You don't believe you will be the judge? Here's how. It's not that you will be king, and anything you say goes. It will be more like... a group of people watching an instant replay on TV. Fans on both sides watch the replay then usually agree what happened during the play because it's obvious to everyone.

As judge, the person that judged harshly in life will get exactly the same in the next life. If you refused to judge people during your lifetime, you won't be judged in the afterlife. Simple and PERFECT... short and sweet. Is that perfect, or WHAT? You, judge, will reside in one or the other, Heaven or hell, whichever justice requires.

WHAT HAPPENS TO REPEAT EVIL DOERS?

Nobody alive is perfect. That said, the answer to the question about repeat evil doers is, that depends. It will be plain to see whether or not you strove for goodness in your lifetime. Some of those people will qualify for Heaven. The rest? It's off to the outer darkness, the Void, where you can do all the evil you want... and a TON you don't want... to yourself. The same kind you dished out in life. Forever.

WHAT IS PERFECT JUSTICE?

There is perfect justice waiting in the next life. Do you know what that means?? People who caused intentional suffering will pay. What should happen to these people? As usual, the answer is perfect and simple. They will be on the receiving end of the evil they've done to others, only it's intensified and multiplied, because they'll know it will never end. For every single time we were put in fear, or lied to, or injured physically or mentally, there WILL be justice.

How does this make you feel... I'VE ALWAYS KNOWN YOU ARE BEYOND STUPID!! I CAN'T BELIEVE THE AMOUNT OF STUPID GOD WAS ABLE TO RAM INTO THAT NASTY BODY OF YOURS... Remember how that felt for a second. Because every time during life that you say something mean to someone, starting at the life review, YOU become the target of your meanness! You WILL feel exactly as bad as you made them feel, and worse. If you don't make the cut, it could last FOREVER. That sounds EXACTLY like PERFECT JUSTICE to me. It's simple. It's perfect. ...How will you be treating yourself when you arrive??

Here is some more Perfect Justice for you. You will be forgiven EXACTLY as you forgave during your life! Somebody let that cat out of the bag a couple thousand years ago! Well, it's true.

Remember that grudge you've been holding? What grudge? ...That's better.

...BUT I HAVE A THOUSAND QUESTIONS

Note... When meeting your Maker, all talking is mental, mind-to-mind, and unimaginably FAR faster than the speed of normal thought, SUPER-HYPER-FAST, and PERFECTLY understood. There are NO misunderstandings, and the Truth will come out unimaginably faster than instantly!

Suddenly, the subject turned to going back or staying there... wherever there was. There were Bobby's younger brothers still at home that would be left alone, if he stays... they're with their mother, who is alone. Should he stay? Should he leave?

Then, something changed. There was a brain "tug", as if he was being pulled away. Something was telling him that he was going to go back. "But I have a THOUSAND questions!", Bobby quickly blurts out. He's told, "You will have the answer to your thousand questions.".

"I'll tell the whole world", said Bobby. "You can't do it.", was the reply. "I can DO it.", he says. My brother, Angelboy will help. Bobby had taught him addition and subtraction AND was beginning multiplication when the lad was just five years old, before he even got to school, so school would be a cinch for him (one less hard class!). ("NOBODY" else did that, back then.) Angelboy, who he all but raised while their mother worked two, sometimes three jobs. Apparently, the job Bobby did "raising" him left something to be desired.

Angelboy was the same kid that looked forward to ratting

out Bobby for the smallest house rules infractions... but, somehow, he never got punched in his head for doing it (...maybe he should have been, huh? Maybe that's what was done wrong.). Bobby was actually ARGUING with Jesus (!!) saying that Angelboy would not only believe when told of the death experience, he'd want to help in any way he could. WRONG and WRONG.

"Surely mom would believe me." The reply received? "No." "Well, my uncle, who I'm a clone of ...we almost share a brain... he'll believe me and help, if it's needed." What was the answer that came back? Jesus again just said, "No.". "Well then... I can do it alone, if I have to.", Bobby said. "Most people will think you're crazy, talking about this." "Fine. Let them say whatever they want to about me, it won't stop me!", Bobby tells Jesus. All this in... one second? Less?

Bobby was told many things. One was about his not wanting to leave this life when his time came, and it was quite unbelievable to him. There were a LOT of things like that ... which only added to the wonder and confusion. Life as a teenager was pure hell. (I'd give details... but hate to make people cry.) It absolutely seemed like life would only get worse and worse right up until the end. Not wanting to just get outta' here, at the appointed time, seemed impossible. Wrong again.

Then there's this one. There was going to be so much to do, at the appointed time for the return trip to eternity, that it couldn't possibly all be done. At the time of the telling, there was nothing BUT time to kill so, that was really hard to believe. Now that the time is approaching, that looks to be coming true as well.

RETURN TO THE WRECK SITE

The next thing you know, Bobby was flying down a tunnel. A pit to nowhere, or...? As it turns out, almost instantly it was back to the wrecked car and back into his aching body, feeling the pain of his injuries, but also feeling confused. Head aching from hitting the windshield, chest hurting from bending the steering wheel down, all the way around... He didn't remember much about the experience immediately afterward.

Got to get out of the car... shift into "park"... but... the gear shifter is gone. (It's with the transmission, laying on the ground.) Forget the shifter, get out that door... the one where the handle doesn't do anything. (The pickup swung around and wrecked the mechanism when it hit the drivers' door.) Fine. Roll it down and get out the window... except it won't roll down. (The window shattered, so there's nothing there to roll down.) Is the passenger out cold? No, he's disappeared! He was there just a second ago. Wait. The passenger door is open! Get out of there. Where is the passenger? Inside the building, calling for help, hopefully. Bobby eventually goes inside too.

Sure enough, the call for help is being made. Their eyes meet. His friends' eyes get huge! Bobby inquires, "What?". The reply comes back, "You were dead!". Bobby says, "WHAT?", not exactly comprehending what that meant. He says it again, in disbelief, "YOU were DEAD!", and this guy would know. Unable to see how that could have been true, Bobby pauses, now even MORE confused, then says, "Well, I'm NOT dead NOW!", and they both went out to wait for the emergency vehicles.

DEADLY DETAILS

Quite a bit later, while walking through the park with his brother, something was said about dying... when this... recall... wave... is what he called it, came over him, and suddenly he remembered a tremendous number of details about his death, and that it had ALREADY HAPPENED! He had DETAILS! A LOT of details and the whole thing was almost beyond words! It was then that Bobby knew he actually HAD experienced something incredible because of the wreck.

It took Bobby a long time to process what had happened. He struggled to find words to describe his death experience, but he knew that it had changed him in profound ways. He no longer feared death... or anything else, knowing that there absolutely was something beyond this life. He felt a sense of peace, having seen that there WILL be Justice in the end... and purpose, knowing that he had been given a chance to do... something really good.

The man he had been before the accident seemed like a stranger to him now. He had seen something that he could not explain, something that had given him a new perspective on life. Bobby felt like he was beginning to understand life in a way he never had before.........and he had gotten answers to most of his long-held questions, and even some he didn't know he had. Most importantly, he also knew that everything would be okay, no matter what happened next because there will be Justice. THINK ABOUT THAT. ...In the end, everything would be OK, no matter what happened next... or after that... OR after that...

EVERYTHING CHANGED!

The experience completely changed his perspective. Having begun questioning everything he had once taken for granted, he also realized that there was more to life than what he was living.

Over the next several months, Bobby found himself constantly thinking about his experience and his priorities in life. He began to build a new life for himself, taking risks and pursuing his passions. He also formed deeper connections with people than he had ever done before.

From then on, he dedicated himself to sharing his experience with others, to help them to find their own sense of purpose, knowing that everything will be OK, no matter what happens next. Now he takes the memory of that experience with him everywhere he goes, knowing that it has permanently changed him in previously unimaginable ways.

It is important to mention the profound impact that these experiences can have on individuals and the potential for positive transformation. Although the experience was mystifying, this near-death experience was a catalyst for a new beginning. He had been given a new sense of direction and purpose.

"Why You"?

People that hear of his experience often ask WHY this happened to Bobby. Why wasn't it the preacher's kid or the banker's kid? What was so special about Bob? Nothing we can see. He does like to help people. He LOVES justice and fairness. Also, it was just about all he talked about... he wanted a face to face with Jesus. Could he really have gotten it?? One thing about it, he'd be the first one to talk about it, if he DID. Maybe THAT is why......! Bobby said to remember that an NDE can happen to anybody... even you!

Sure, there will always be people who refuse to believe it... He thinks of them like this... compared to eternity, this life is just a SPECK... a SPECK on a SPECK! That means the naysayers will be gone in a SPECK of time, AND they will be gone forever! Bob says, "No worries! ... I can't MAKE anyone believe what they don't want to believe.".

One relative wouldn't even discuss the death experience. He threw the phone down and ran for the prayer closet. His wife began describing the clinical reasons why Bobby must be ...a NUT. OK. Bobby's major in high school AND college was psychology. He knew something about the subject and knew better. ...There had been a warning that there would be huge resistance, once returned to life. Jesus was right, can you believe it (tongue in cheek)!?

Bobby tried talking to them about his NDE again a bit later. The guy's wife talked about how memories change, but she was still not willing to listen to the details of the experience. Having written at length about the NDE just after the event, there were a few minor details added later, as there always are, but ZERO major changes. Naturally he thinks Bob's changed his story! What are all these extra details?? They're... EXTRA DETAILS! Well, why didn't you tell us before?? Really?? Maybe because you wouldn't listen long enough to hear additional details... back then either?!! You just ran to the prayer closet. Wow. There is NO doubt that his wife and he WOULD listen to details about a trip to somewhere like... Disneyworld... which could be described in a similar fashion. Why not this? Or are they scared they might both be convinced to become an amusement park "mouse"?? Bobby didn't expect such closed-mindedness from his own family.

Imagine a trip to one of those HUGE amusement parks. It can be fun, exciting and relaxing. There are lots of games, rides and shows, often for one price. You've planned just such a trip with a friend of yours, but at the last second, you can't go. Your friend finds someone else to go with, and returns with tales of excitement, happiness and entertainment bliss. There were friendly people. The weather was PERFECT. Your friend reports completely forgetting the stress and strife of life. It seems that everyone that goes there doesn't want to go back home! The ones that do return home agree to meet back at the park SOON.

Was this tale too **SCARY** to listen to? Can you believe your friend? Has this friend ever told a grandiose lie to you before? No? Sure, why not believe him? Nice story? What's the point? What a coincidence (tongue in cheek). It's exactly like the description of a trip to the afterlife. Come to think of it... the prayer closet crowd could be told the amusement park story, then later reveal it to be a metaphor for the near-death experience!

DON'T TALK ABOUT IT

There have been a few, "answers can't just come to you!" negative comments. It was suggested that nobody be told of the death experience. "Surely, we are meant to keep talk of God to ourselves, until somebody asks us (about our perfect life??)", was suggested. I don't see it happening! Who has a perfect life?? I want names.

"You can't live your life by a vision" is definitely a popular reply. (...Wait a second. What did St. Paul do? Saw a vision and switched sides!) ...Close family has gone to great lengths to stop this line of discussion. HOW COULD ANYBODY DO THAT? One person especially set in her ways even quoted non-existent... non-existent ...Bible verses as proof that...a man who leaves his home and family to talk to people about this is no better than a heathen, blah, blah, blah. The chapter and verse couldn't be named, because it doesn't exist.

Bobby felt strongly that this isn't something you keep to yourself. After all, it concerns the most important topic of a persons' lifetime. He said that most people he talks to agree... IF SOMEONE SAYS THEY'VE LEARNED THINGS FROM JESUS, PEOPLE WANT TO HEAR IT and decide for themselves what to believe. NOT telling everyone you know is like having the next winning lotto numbers and keeping it to yourself!

Bobby says he would love it if the naysayers were in his shoes. What would they do with this experience... nothing? So, they're yella'. Or they've already decided. Making final decisions without listening to all the facts sounds like it's the result of a weak or closed mind... a mind made up... a mind that, when it's wrong, STAYS wrong!

PROVE IT TO ME

Imagine this scenario: You have never been to a casino before, and you're not fond of losing money, but you decide to check it out anyway. Upon arrival, you walk around and briefly observe the different games before abruptly leaving.

Someone might say, "I want every detail so I can go, play and win. How does roulette work? What is the best bet? How about blackjack? Craps?" However, you respond, "How could I possibly know everything about those? I was only there for a few moments." The same thing can be said by someone who has had a near-death experience.

People who have had a (near) death experience do not suddenly gain all knowledge and become perfect beings. However, if they have the courage to speak out about their experience, they may be able to shed some light on what happened. After such an experience, there are many questions that arise, such as: What just happened? Was it real? What does it all mean? Should I say anything about it or keep it to myself?

Unfortunately, some people may call those who speak out about their experience liars or even crazy. Despite this, some people like Bobby have the courage to share their story saying, "I could hardly believe it... and it happened to me!" What did he have for evidence... a multitude of insights... and...

Living up north, he worked outside, occasionally until it was fifty degrees below zero, Fahrenheit. He just dressed for it. Maybe the fingers or nose would get cold, but it virtually never caused goosebumps. Bobby was always the last to put on a jacket when winter set in. At the end of winter, guess who is the first to wear shorts. Bobby just DOESN'T get goosebumps... EXCEPT when talking about the death experience! That's right. It can be ninety degrees, and he'll get goosebumps talking about this, every time. Not just goosebumps, goosebumps in places people don't normally get goosebumps. It was concerning that, having come back to "life", he'd have absolutely no proof of the death experience, but there WERE all these questions with answers he's not smart enough to know... AND goosebumps!

For years Bobby said very little about the death experience. Immediately afterward there were NO WORDS to describe it anyway... figure that out! It took multiple years just to find words BIG enough to BEGIN to describe it! That is, until a chance conversation with Mary.

Mary was one of Bobby's coworkers. She was reading a book, in her spare time. Bobby asked what she was reading. She said it was a book by Moody called "Life after Life". She said it was about someone dead flying through a tunnel at great speed and... He cut her off. He mentioned that after the tunnel you stop in a pitch-black place. Next there's a bright light... She cut him off. "So, you've read the book?", she asked. Now he had to tell her. Bobby said, "No, it happened to me!". That was the first retelling (after the brothers' rejection. It had been years since that rejection happened.) of many. The secret was out.

TELL EVERYBODY!

Those people that said, "keep it to yourself" are the same folks that said not to talk to people who want to talk about Heaven, when they come to the door. The KITY (keep it to yourself) crowd are afraid they might "influence" people. ...If a person modifies their beliefs, it would be for something that is BETTER, wouldn't it?

Don't talk with the doorknockers? The best way to personally make anything known may be going door to door. Besides, God brought them right to your door and you ARE going to talk with them. Just maybe one of you will learn something important. That is, unless you already HAVE the perfect religion... You've never been wrong either, I presume. Let me guess, you thought that you were wrong one time long ago, but you were mistaken?

If having set beliefs is good for you, how are set beliefs NOT good for the doorknockers? If they have to be able to believe new things, by coming over to your beliefs, how is it not the same for you? If the WHOLE truth is ever to be found, all possibilities must be considered by everyone. It looks like the doorknockers win this round.

WAS IT A DREAM?

Even before the NDE, one of the things this kid dreamed about when he went to sleep at night was flying... without an airplane. How do I know? **I AM the kid, "Bobby".**

The first time the flying happened, it was impossible to stay asleep. With the first downward move I was WIDE awake! It was GREAT, flying. Out there... free as a... Well, you know. Next time sleep-flying, hopefully it would be nothing BUT flying... none of that... plummeting toward Earth. That will wake you up quick.

When the flying happened again, so did the plummeting. (The "old wives' tale was then tested where, if you hit the ground in the dream, you die. No, you don't die.) After bouncing off the ground twice, flying became easy. All hesitancy was gone. As it turns out, not only can flying be controlled, BUT EVERYTHING in a dream can be controlled. It's called "lucid dreaming". That's actually one thing I don't have to convince people of, that it's possible... just that it happens with me. One down, dozens left to go.

Since realizing that controlling dreams was possible, it has helped people I know control nightmares. Some have learned how to STAY asleep, when it is desired. Example? Dreaming you're having a talk with a deceased loved one.

How is it done? The first thing that must be done is to realize you're dreaming. Is ANYTHING at all happening that is impossible or, there's no reason you would be doing that thing... like, I don't know... jumping a canyon on a unicycle. In this case I might "create" myself some wings to take away the feeling of danger. (I want to keep flying, not wake up.) If I was feeling a bit spry, I might create an elephant that is being ridden... who sprouts wings! I'm not kidding! But then, I've been doing it for a long while. That kind of control could take decades to achieve, but it is DEFINITELY possible.

The point is, NO, it was NOT a dream. Everything in the next life is so... REAL. It's EASY to tell the difference... You'll see, either way you go.

Personally, I know where I was. Where else might you be told BY JESUS that, for the rest of your life, people would be trying to prove that this NDE never happened, or it was something else? Even with tons of evidence. Where else can you see every second of your life, even ones you've forgotten about, all in ...five (?) seconds? Yeah, you'll know.

ABOUT DEATH
Was Death Painful?

It's common for people to expect that death is painful. This isn't about "dying", where there may be physical pain or discomfort for days as the body shuts down. It's about the moment we leave our bodies... death.

During a near-death experience, people report a sense of detachment from their physical body, which can include a lack of physical sensation, including pain. If there was pain during my NDE, it went completely unnoticed.

It's also worth noting that many people who have had near-death experiences report a sense of peace, and love during their experience.

WHAT IS DEATH LIKE?

When most people think about death, they think about the pain we're likely to be in, just before we expire. They think about the sorrow of friends and family that will suddenly be left without them. Death sounds like a real bummer. ...People have that all wrong!

Think of a time when you are dreaming. It seems pretty real. Suddenly you're awake. At first you may feel... disjointed in time or confused. You try to remember what you were doing LAST. THAT is what death is like. It will be a tremendous strain to remember what you were doing at the moment you passed! You may not remember AT ALL. I didn't.

You don't FEEL any different. You're YOU. Pain? What pain?? It doesn't matter HOW you died, it's just the same. You will be overjoyed! NO problem from "life" matters anymore... assuming certain things are true.

Have you ever broken a finger or toe? How worried are you RIGHT NOW about that long ago completely mended toe? How much time each day do you sit thinking about that once broken toe? You barely even remember it, if at all, huh? There is just no reason to think about it! THAT is what death is like, once it's done. It's also nothing to fear, if you're not a rotten individual who leaves suffering in their wake.

WHAT HAPPENS WHEN WE DIE?

The body stops functioning and the brain ceases activity, which typically results in death. Beyond that has been a matter of speculation. Many religions believe in an afterlife. Some believe that the soul goes to a specific place based on actions during their lifetime.

People have reported near-death experiences where individuals report experiencing a variety of sensations, such as peace, joy, and a sense of connection to a divine presence. This was the case with my experience.

WHAT HAPPENS AFTER WE DIE?

Some believe in an afterlife, while others believe in reincarnation, and still others believe in simply ceasing to exist. Somebody is in for a BIG surprise.

An afterlife may take different forms depending on the individual's actions during their lifetime. For example, in Christianity, it is believed that the soul goes to either Heaven or hell.

People who have had near-death experiences report a sense of peace and calm, as well as a feeling of being surrounded by light or loved ones who have already passed away. Others report vivid experiences of visiting other dimensions. The first thing I got was a quick trip to what I called the "waiting place".

WHAT HAPPENS TO OUR CONSCIOUSNESS WHEN WE PASS ON?

The nature of consciousness is still not entirely understood. Some theories suggest that consciousness arises from the complex interactions of neurons in the brain, and it ceases to exist once the brain stops functioning after death. Man is that WRONG, from what I saw. However, there are also theories that consciousness may exist beyond the physical body, such as in the form of quantum consciousness. Christianity proposes Heaven and hell, where the consciousness goes to a place of reward or punishment.

WHERE DO WE GO RIGHT AFTER DEATH?

In Christianity it is believed that after death, the soul is judged and sent to either Heaven or hell. Some people believe that after death the soul remains on Earth as a ghost or spirit, while others believe that the soul simply ceases to exist. During my near-death experience, first I took a trip to the land of nothing good... the "waiting place".

DOES EVERYONE GO TO HEAVEN?

Not a chance. That death experience proved that there most definitely IS an afterlife, and a life review... which was HIGHLY critical of shortcomings. It felt at the time like possibly NO ONE goes to Heaven! That is, until it was shown the simplicity with which it is achieved! If we love everyone and treat everyone the way we want to be treated ourselves, that goes a long way towards you being approved for that Heavenly address.

HEAVEN, CAN WE CHOOSE TO GO NOW?

I'm afraid not. I look at it like this... The boss has sent us here to do a job. If the job doesn't get done, what was the use of having us here, alive? Also, because leaving life on your schedule would tell God that you don't give a damn about His schedule. Not a good idea, Dunsel.

IS THERE A GOOD PLACE AND A BAD PLACE WHERE PEOPLE GO FOR ETERNITY?

Well, yeah. You WON'T believe the difference between them! You may only get a whiff of them during an NDE, but that is PLENTY, and it makes the choice simple. One place has every good thing that you can imagine, in multiples and forever. The other place... just thinking about it sucks a little life out of me. It has ZERO good things, worse than you can imagine, by the ship load AND forever. ...I'll bet you that, within a minute in this particular place, you're screaming... forever. BET ME. ...I don't lose many bets. I only bet when I'm going to win.

WHAT MAKES THOSE PLACES GOOD AND BAD?

Heaven is seen as a place of eternal joy because it is believed to be in the presence of God, who is the source of all goodness and love. Those who have lived a life in accordance with God's teachings are granted entry to Heaven, where they will be reunited with loved ones who have also passed on.

On the other hand, hell is seen as a place of eternal suffering because it is a state of complete separation from God and all that is good. Those who have lived a life of repeated and unrepentant nastiness (sin) are sent to "hell", where they will experience eternal separation from God and anything good... like light and people and everything else.

...RETURNED...

Heaven and hell are fundamental to the faith. Heaven is the eternal abode of the faithful, while hell (or the Void) is the place of eternal punishment for the wicked. After leading a righteous life, people will be rewarded with eternal happiness and bliss in Heaven. However, if they succumb to choosing to do evil, they risk eternal torment.

Although no one can prove they've returned from either of these places to give a firsthand account, I know that they exist. For me, these places are not just abstract ideas, but a reality that I expect to experience after my death.

Those glimpses of Heaven and hell seen during the near-death experience remind me to strive towards living a virtuous life and to avoid temptation. It has also given me the impossible... PEACE, knowing that there is a place of eternal peace and happiness waiting for us after we leave this world.

WHY DIDN'T SOMEBODY TELL ME?

Now that you have heard about the actual existence of the afterlife, it is up to you to use this knowledge. No longer can you get to the Judgement and claim you didn't know... nobody told you. ...It's like the game of "tag"... and you're "it".

The afterlife is a huge part of many religions around the world. Accepting this can help you live a more meaningful life. It is never too late to strive towards living a more virtuous life. It's important to make the most of the time you have left in this world, to do good and help others, and to prepare yourself for the afterlife... now that you HAVE been told.

ABOUT THE AFTERLIFE

Don't be surprised if the answers given here do not align with your assumptions about the afterlife. MANY of the answers coming from the (near) death experience didn't align with mine either.

How Does Time Work in the Afterlife?

Eternity can be difficult to grasp from our human perspective, since it is bound by time. The act of moving from NOW, until... NOW implies moving through time, while we're alive. How that action is accomplished in the afterlife WITHOUT moving through time... is unknown. Instead of me being disappointed by that, maybe it is actually evidence that "Bobby" WAS no longer physically, "matter", or even NEAR matter, as that NDE happened, eh? Many people who have had near-death experiences (NDEs) report a sense of timelessness and eternity in the afterlife. One thing is sure, there is NO TIME in the afterlife. THAT is how "forever" can exist. Simple. Perfect.

Eternity does not mean an infinite amount of time, but rather outside of time altogether. Where there's no time, there's eternity. In this state, there is no beginning or end, no past or future, but rather a sense of being fully present in the eternal Now. In which case, our interstellar travel capsules COULD all be dropped at once and DONE. ALSO, loved ones who have passed WON'T have "time" to miss us! This ALL fits together. Are you following this?

Is There Really an "Afterlife"?

The answer to this question is a real game changer. Once we're positive that there IS an afterlife, it makes decisions IN life easier to make. Most of the world believes there is an afterlife. The main things they disagree on are the details.

Is "The End" Really "THE" End?

That was a no-brainer, at this point... No, we continue on, after "life" is done. There is NO END at all, EVER. That changes everything, doesn't it? Just to KNOW that there's no end. So, we don't cease to exist at the time that we call "death"? Not a chance. Not even if you want it that way. During the NDE it was shown that everyone continues on after death.

IS THERE AN AFTERLIFE FOR EVERYONE, OR JUST SOME PEOPLE?

In many religions, it is believed that the afterlife is determined by a person's actions during their life. For example, Christianity. They believe they'll have eternal life in Heaven, while those who do not will face eternal punishment. In Islam, it is believed that one's good and bad deeds will be weighed on a scale on Judgment Day, determining whether they will go to Paradise or hell. In this near-death experience, it was shown that both interpretations of the end result were valid. According to the NDE, nobody ceases to exist after death.

DO WE HAVE A PHYSICAL BODY IN THE AFTERLIFE?

The near-death experience suggests that we do have a form of physical body in the afterlife, but it is not composed of matter, as were our physical bodies on Earth. The spiritual body in the death experience was made of energy or light. It certainly looked like light... or plasma... but "solid". See the problems I've had all these years, describing ...the unknown... the non-understood of the NDE?

What Is the Nature of the Afterlife?

Some believe that there is a physical body in the afterlife, but it is not made of matter in the traditional sense. Rather, it is a spiritual body that is more akin to energy or light. This spiritual body is believed to be eternal and not subject to the physical laws of our world. The afterlife is often associated with feelings of love, wellness, gratefulness, and happiness, as well as a sense of oneness. However, the Void or place of punishment, is devoid of ANYTHING good.

WHAT EFFECT DO EXPECTATIONS HAVE?

It appears that the expectations we have in this life do not have a direct impact on our experience of the afterlife. The consequences of actions in this life will be judged regardless of what we expect. It is important to make decisions that align with your principles. The reason is actions and choices during life will determine our experience in the afterlife.

Are We STILL OURSELVES After Death?

We are the same in the next life that we always were in this life. We don't magically change at death into someone... more acceptable... either. It seems that most people think about Heaven as a place where everybody's super nice, and nobody ever gives anybody a hassle, but if we didn't LIVE that way, we're not going to be that way in the next life and should not expect to see Heaven. No, we don't need to be perfect, but it will be easy to see whether "good" was what we strove for or not because, by then, we've HAD our chance to prove who we really ARE, by the way we were in life. If it was not... well... the only alternative is nothing good.

DO WE RETAIN OUR IDENTITY AND INDIVIDUALITY?

Many belief systems agree, we are still ourselves after death. The soul and identity continue on after death, from what I saw during the death experience. Our consciousness remains intact.

You've heard that people often see loved ones who have already passed, during a (near) death experience? If you weren't "you" after death, how would anyone recognize lost loved ones, meaning you? I have no information on how to recognize loved ones who are now toads... or grasshoppers and such...

Also, individuality? If the way you lived allowed you into Heaven, your individuality is unchanged. The "riffraff" goes "away". The good are just as they always were. You don't become just one more angel in a row.

IS THE AFTERLIFE A PLACE, A STATE OF MIND, OR SOMETHING ELSE ENTIRELY?

The afterlife is difficult to describe, as I've said. Many people believe that the afterlife is something else entirely beyond our current understanding. If you ask me, that's right. When the NDE first happened, it took months and months for me to put just ONE sentence together in an attempt to describe just one aspect of the experience! For one, there was no "matter" there that I was aware of. ...It is definitely "something else". INSIDE Heaven, who knows.

IS THE AFTERLIFE A PERMANENT STATE, OR CAN WE MOVE ON FROM IT?

The afterlife is definitely a permanent state, with no return to earthly life likely. The spirit of the deceased moves on to an eternity in Heaven or hell, according to the NDE.

CAN WE FIND PEACE IN THE AFTERLIFE?

What I was shown was that the afterlife is a place of eternal peace and happiness, away from the struggles and strife of this life.

If we consider the viewpoint that the afterlife is a realm of peace and happiness, then the question becomes one of how we can reach that state. Live a life of love. Don't hate. The rest will come. A loving attitude is key to finding peace and happiness in the afterlife. This is a common belief across many religions that believe in the importance of treating others with kindness, compassion, and love. People also believe that doing good deeds, performing acts of charity, can help one attain peace and happiness in the afterlife.

Some may find comfort in the idea of a peaceful afterlife, while others may find it more helpful to focus on living a fulfilling and meaningful life in the present. Whether we can find peace and happiness in the afterlife may never be fully answered, down here, but by living a life of love, we can create a more peaceful, better world in the here and now.

IS THERE A WAY TO COMMUNICATE WITH THE AFTERLIFE?

Scientifically speaking, there is no evidence to support the idea that communication with those in the afterlife is possible. However, many people have reported experiences that they interpret as messages from loved ones who have passed away, such as dreams or signs that seem to be directly associated with the deceased.

Many religious traditions also offer practices that are said to make possible communication with the afterlife, such as prayer or meditation.

One argument against the possibility is based on people who have had near-death experiences (NDEs). Many NDEs, such as this one, report feeling a sense of peace and connectedness during their experience, but few, including this one, report actually communicating with deceased loved ones.

The question remains unresolved. Though there is no definite answer, many people find comfort in the idea that their loved ones might still be with them in some form, even after death.

CAN WE COMMUNICATE WITH THE LIVING FROM THE AFTERLIFE?

Many people believe in the possibility of such communication and report personal experiences that they interpret as messages or signs from deceased loved ones. There is no solid evidence of it. Even so, some people claim to have connected with the deceased.

People are happy to think that their loved ones may still be with them. Others remain skeptical. I've seen some odd occurrences SINCE the NDE. It seems... it may be possible to communicate. One example...it has yet to be PROVEN where the information comes from that allows the foresight spoken of in the book, "No Doubt, You Were DEAD!" also about this NDE and ESP. That is TBD.

Are There "Signs" HERE for Us to See?

Ever since returning to life, there's been a lingering question about... it seems as though there are actually "hints" around us during our lives. I did not believe this was possible... until after the NDE. They come in many forms. During the life review it was AMAZING to see that they were there the entire time but were seldom noticed... EVEN though I had always been on the lookout for exactly that. ...I wish I could describe it better. ...This has been a problem from the start... describing what I barely understood.

Ha! Got one! Right when I needed it. This weekend I got roped into listening to a "60-90" minute turned to three-hour timeshare sales pitch. This poor salesman had a serious heart problem. He was due to have open-heart surgery in weeks but called it off. Afterward, he spoke to his clergyman and was told to read from a certain book of the Bible, and suggested he gets a second opinion. Also, to not be afraid of death. Sure.
Later, while dining out, he met a woman that was everything he was looking for in a mate. They got together. She had the same name as the book of the Bible that was suggested he read. That's unusual.

He calls his general practitioner for a referral to a second specialist. The name he gets? It's the same as the Bible book, and the new (hopefully) girlfriend.

He realizes the name game is going on when he's stuck in slow moving traffic, behind a semi with one word on the back of the trailer. Right! He gets his phone camera, he starts recording while talking about the situation when, even though traffic was barely moving, and he was maybe two car lengths behind that semi, all of a sudden, a car FLIES in between him and the semi. The camera refocuses on the newly closest thing. It's one of those new brands of car... with the same name as the semi, the referred doctor, the girl, and the referred Bible book! GENESIS! Something is going on HERE. FIVE with the UNUSUAL name, in less than a week, each right after speaking about the upcoming heart surgery! If there was ever a case of a message from beyond, this MUST be one.

What's the rest of the story? Affected by the "signs"... he's having the procedure done at the new place. The new place specializes in his problem, and they do it through a vein (artery?) which took a LOAD off his mind. He should have a MUCH better experience skipping open-heart.

DO WE HAVE A CHOICE WHETHER TO STAY?

As was shown to me, the afterlife is a place of judgment, where the deeds of our lives are weighed, and we are assigned a place, based on our actions during life. Our choices during life determine our experience in the afterlife. In some cases, presumably not every time, they may be given a chance to return to life.

CAN WE CHOOSE OUR OWN DESTINY?

...We have a choice through our actions, not predetermined by outside factors, such as fate or divine intervention, while we are alive. In this way, our choices in life influence how we experience the afterlife.

Our destiny in the afterlife is determined based on factors such the deeds of our lives. In this view, we may have limited agency or control over our destiny, as it is largely shaped by factors outside of our control, once we are IN the afterlife. Many religious practices are said to enable us to shape our destiny in the afterlife, such as prayer and good deeds.

I always wondered if the idea of judgment in the afterlife was just a way to encourage ethical behavior in the masses.

IS THERE A WAY TO AVOID THE AFTERLIFE ALTOGETHER?

WHO would want to?? Somebody that hates everything and everybody, maybe. Somebody that lives to make others suffer. Little do they know that they are just feathering their own bed... but it's never too late to change. **No, there is NO way to avoid the next life. IT'S THE MAIN EVENT!!**

CAN WE CHOOSE TO RETURN TO OUR BODY AFTER EXPERIENCING THE AFTERLIFE?

It's true that some people who have had near-death experiences (NDEs) report being given a choice... to return to their physical body or to continue on in the afterlife.

During an NDE, a person will experience a sense of leaving their physical body and entering a different "existence". This can include meeting spiritual beings, being outside of time, and a feeling of overwhelming love and peace.

In some cases, a person may be given a choice to return to their body and continue their existence on Earth. This choice may be presented to them by a spiritual being, or it may be from a sense of knowing. Not everyone who has an NDE is given a choice to return, and not everyone who is given a choice chooses to return.

HOW DO NDE'S RELATE TO THE AFTERLIFE?

Near-death experiences (NDEs) are glimpses into the afterlife. Many people who have had NDEs report encountering angels or deceased loved ones and experiencing a sense of peace and love. Some NDEs have descriptions of a heavenly environments, beautiful landscapes, colors, and music.

The similarities between NDEs reported by people from different beliefs suggest that there are universal elements. NDEs may not provide proof positive of the afterlife, but they DO offer a view of what is waiting for us beyond this life.

CAN WE REVISIT PAST LIVES FROM THE AFTERLIFE?

The question of whether we can revisit past lives while in the afterlife must be answered in the negative. Just wait until YOU travel quadrillions of miles per hour, then tell me you are going ANYWHERE else, on your own, and I won't believe it. It's too far out. The "Good Place"... nobody wants to leave. It's really far out too!

DO WE EXPERIENCE PAIN IN THE AFTERLIFE?

According to the NDE, there is an afterlife, with one realm of joy and bliss (Heaven) and another realm of suffering and pain (hell). One's afterlife experience is determined by their actions during their lifetime, such as was shown during the NDE. Be ready.

CAN WE BE REBORN?

In beliefs that hold a dualistic afterlife view, reincarnation isn't a possibility. The afterlife is a final destination, where the soul or consciousness remains in a particular state of being for eternity.

CAN WE EXPERIENCE DIFFERENT DIMENSIONS?

That may be exactly what the next life IS. There is no scientific evidence to support the existence of multiple dimensions in the afterlife. I am not sure how to accurately describe WHERE I was, except to say, it's far out, too! It's another unsure/unknown.

ABOUT LOVE
What is the True Nature of Love?

There is no single definition of love that can include all of the nuances and aspects that are associated with love.

Love is an intense feeling of affection as well as a deep sense of caring for the well-being of the other. True love is often demonstrated through acts of kindness, and selflessness towards another person. Love is also an action... or a behavior... like supporting them through difficult times or making sacrifices for their benefit. Love is often a sense of connection with the other or being "in sync" with the other person.

Love can also be challenging and difficult. Love is often revealed in how we respond to these challenges and how we strive to maintain connections with others, brother.

HOW CAN WE HAVE A PERSONAL RELATIONSHIP WITH GOD?

Really? How can we have anything other than a personal relationship?? This isn't a party line. The evidence of a personal relationship? I've never had anyone try to cut in, in the middle of one of our "conversations" (prayers)... have you? God loves every single one of us... LIKE WE ARE THE ONLY PERSON THAT EVER LIVED. EVERRR. You don't get more personal than that!

HELP IF YOU CAN

It may seem unfair, but we are expected to be our brothers' keeper to a certain degree. While some people may perform good deeds solely for the purpose of gaining recognition, true love and kindness towards others are what matter in the end.

Many people have a surplus of material possessions that could be redirected to them. Some people already demonstrate genuine care for others through their actions, however, excessive and unnecessary spending on luxurious items such as an eight-passenger gas-guzzling vehicle, a huge boat, or an extravagant home may be considered a waste of divine resources in the end. When our time on earth is over, such extravagance will be used as evidence against us. Remember, this life is just a speck on a speck compared to forever. Get forever right.

LOOKING FOR LOVE

Eventually, the idea arose that answers I was left searching for might be found in just a few words, but even with a short list of potential answers, the list still seemed too long. As the idea continued to be knocked around, it seemed possible that only a single word was needed to answer most of life's questions. This notion seemed absurd, but it felt right.

Several months later, a friend came to visit, proudly showing off pictures of his new baby daughter. As he began to speak, "I sure do...", the answer suddenly came to me. "LOVE! THAT is the answer" to the thousand questions. The answer had been there all along. I had written and spoken the answer many times before: Exactly what was said during the NDE was, "You will have the ANSWER" - not "answers" - "to your thousand questions." It was a profound realization.

DOES MY DECEASED LOVED ONE MISS ME?

Once you've made it "up there", it is perfectly clear that God DOES exist, and there IS Justice in the "end", AND everyone will get a fair shake. Even so, if you are left down here after your loved one has gone on, your first thought may be that they're up there, having a GREAT time, and couldn't care less what's going on "down here". But there's more to it.

Have you seen the movie where the government built a machine that aliens sent them plans for? They assume it's for intergalactic travel, but they aren't sure. A person in a capsule drops through a machine to travel? Well, she drops through. That's all the spectators saw... no travel, nothing. But she said she travelled FAR away (maybe Heaven) and saw her dead father for sixteen minutes. Nobody believes her. (Been there.) In the end, a recording of the event had a blank spot sixteen minutes long.

So, God wanted indisputable proof, to show to each person, of what every individual him/herself is REALLY like. He creates "life", letting everyone make their own choices, when presented with different random events. So, he puts everyone that will ever live into individual "capsules", like in the alien travel device, all at the same time. The time when the capsules are dropping is our lifetime. But in GOD'S "time", the only thing that has changed is that there is now proof of what people are really like inside, for all to see. That way, no one can say that they never got a fair shake.

All this brings us back to the question, does your deceased loved one miss you? I don't think they'll even have time to turn around to look for you, before YOUR time here (Fifty years? Ten?

One hundred?) is up, in the blink of an eye, and you can be reunited!

CRYING FOR OURSELVES!

The NDE showed that extravagant funerals and such are a waste of money. While fancy ceremonies can provide closure for those left behind, they are not "required". The deceased person is already presumably in Heaven, at peace and in a state of bliss, so crying over their passing makes no sense. The person isn't there. They don't know... OR CARE... that you had a huge ceremony in their honor!

People who believe in the afterlife should be happy for their loved ones who have passed on, since they are now healthy and happy and will never suffer again. Those folks left behind, crying and unhappy about their loved ones' departure, appear to be lacking in their belief. They should find comfort in this knowledge, rather than crying and being unhappy for themselves.

FREEDOM FROM FEAR

How Can We Overcome Our Fears and Doubts?

What is that old saying? "Fear fades when Faith appears", I think. That reminds me that once you know that your afterlife is safe, there is no reason to fear death, or anything else. That is exactly why random dogs let me pet them, often when even their owner cannot. If they maim me, no matter what, I only have one lifetime until I'm outta' here, into bliss! What is there to fear? The same goes for being startled. It's hard to startle me. By the time I hear and react, the danger is usually gone.

As far as "doubts" go... Everyone doubts. Doubts lead to the questions that need to be asked in order to solve a problem. Just don't presuppose the worst outcome. It will be alright. In the end, we WIN!

LIVING WITHOUT FEAR?

There is a growing list of things these days that can cause people to fear. Rising housing costs, hospitalizations, vehicle breakdowns, rising food prices, shortages, wildfires, cowardly police ...rabid police, racism, and that's just for starters. Lucky for us our time on earth doesn't have to be fearful.

Why have I never been bitten by a dog, even though I pet everyone I see? Because I'm not afraid. MANY people over the years have FREAKED OUT, just after I'm beginning to pet their dog. "WAIT!" and "HOW ARE YOU DOING THAT?" are common comments. Occasionally there's a "HEY! This is a retired police dog. NOBODY is able to pet him!". I've even gotten a couple, "I can't even pet" him/her!

By learning to manage fear, we can overcome it and live to the fullest. The difference is night and day.

The "WRATH" of God?

As was obvious at the death experience, there is no such thing as the wrath of God.

In fact, the death experience showed that God is an entity of pure love. The idea of God punishing or being angry with individuals is a human projection aimed at God, and it is not possible AT ALL. God is LOVE rolled into an entity. He doesn't hate, or even dislike anyone!

In fact, the death experience tells that God's love is not spread thinly across all of creation. Instead, each individual has a one-on-one with God at all times. In fact, it's as if you were the only person who ever existed, He loves you so much. This understanding can be difficult to grasp while living, for sure. It was PLAIN to see, in person.

HAS ANYONE BEEN HIT IN HEAVEN?

Heaven is understood as a place of peace and harmony. As such, it's unlikely that anyone would ever hit anyone else in Heaven. It would seem unlikely that anyone would engage in ANY form of violence towards others in Heaven. ...And yet, presumably God told Joshua to kill every living thing in the land that would become Israel? No. After the NDE, that is a REAL hard sell. The Old Testament seems to be full of examples where it says God tells us to whack some person or group, usually for doing us wrong. God wouldn't do that! Why? Because there's always hope, I guess. Have you tried asking Him yourself?

ABOUT PRAYER

What is the Purpose of Prayer?

Looking at this from our enlightened viewpoint, the main purpose… is so that the person praying can feel like they now have the attention of the one being prayed TO. Now, having become aware that every thought and every word ever spoken was heard and understood and is easily reviewable, we know that there doesn't have to BE a separate activity, with time set aside to "pray". Plain old "speaking/thinking about" is also heard AND UNDERSTOOD. Besides, God knows what you need before you ask. (You're not one of "those" that only communicates when you want something, are you?)

WHAT IS THE BEST KIND OF PRAYER?

...How happy would it make YOU if your best friend almost never got ahold of you, and when they did, they always "needed" something? They don't contact you, but they have a picture of you on their wall that they look at, on occasion, while thinking about you... for a moment. Feel better? No?

What kind of prayer is the best? Not a "ritual"! Short and sweet... private, one-on-one and continual is best. You could pray only when you need something. You could "pray" to God only before going to bed. You could pray only at a church service. Or you could "SPEAK" to God continuously. ...What would your "bestie" prefer? Contact continuously, no doubt about it. Who do you care more about?? Your best friend or God? Remember before you answer that you WILL hear your answer again, later...

Any thought or conversation, spoken or unspoken toward Heaven (or not!) at any time, in any language will be heard in Heaven. At the life review, every action, ever THOUGHT from an entire lifetime was there for all to see! If we can see it, you KNOW God can see and hear it too. This is no game.

Do We Have to Close Our Eyes When We "Pray"?

You can if you want to. You can also stand on your head... if you want to. At the life review every act and every THOUGHT was there to see. There were absolutely NO comments made at the time, questioning the position I was in. The same goes for kneeling.

DO WE HAVE TO KNEEL WHEN PRAYING?

Obviously not. The best way to "pray" (and/or worship) is constantly. Nobody can kneel virtually all the time and get anything done. No work done, no eating. No eat, no live. No life, no prayers. No prayer... no KNEEL! You'll get plenty of chance to kneel when you are unable to continue standing, in His presence, as happened to me.

RANDOM QUESTIONS AND ANSWERS

The Perfect Religion

There is no such thing as the perfect religion, I'm sorry to say. Some may believe that their particular religion is perfect because it aligns with their personal convictions and brings them peace. Others may see a religion as perfect because of its long history or large following.

The idea that there is a single perfect religion that fits every person's beliefs is unrealistic and, really, impossible. The reality is that religion is a human creation and subject to flaws and imperfections. (YES, yes, yes, God is ABLE to make it perfect, but He doesn't work that way. Oops, I think I just triggered prayer closet time...) Even within a single religion, there are different interpretations that result in divisions. We need to KNOCK IT OFF, thinking that ours is the only "religion" acceptable to God! In this way, they are ALL THE SAME.

Many people find meaning in their religion, but the near-death experience shows that there is more to the spiritual realm than any one religion has been able to fully capture.

It would be more productive to focus on seeking truth than arguing over whose religion is the "best", since it's not perfect. Seeking truth involves being open-minded, questioning assumptions, and listening to differing perspectives. By doing that, we can start to better understand life... this one and the next.

WHY DID GOD CREATE HUMANS?

One possible reason, God is a loving and compassionate being who desires to share His goodness with others. By creating humans, God was able to express His love and goodness.

WHY GIVE HUMANS FREE WILL?

Free will is the ability to make choices independent of any predetermined destiny or fate.

One reason why God may have given us free will is that without free will, we would be unable to face the consequences of our actions. Without the ability to choose freely, we would not be responsible for our actions, since our choices would be predetermined. By giving us free will, God makes us be responsible for our choices and to be held accountable for our actions.

Love, by its very nature, requires the ability to choose freely. God desires a relationship with us, but that relationship must be freely chosen. By giving us free will, God allows us to choose whether to love Him.

WHAT ARE WE SUPPOSED TO BE DOING HERE?

What is the purpose of our existence? If we were living in a perfect world, like the Garden of Eden, our only responsibility would be to enjoy the beauty around us. However, we live in a world where countless people are struggling and require our help. We are all brothers and sisters, and when one of our siblings requires assistance, it is our duty to offer them our support.

Love is the most valuable gift one can give and receive, especially from a divine perspective. The joy that comes with such a gift is indescribable. Once we have love in our hearts, caring for others will come naturally. Help those in need whenever we can. Really, by doing that, we are not only assisting others, but we are also helping ourselves.

WHAT IS THE MEANING OF LIFE?

Some people find meaning in their careers, relationships, or creative pursuits, while others find meaning through their experiences of nature, art, or travel.

From a religious perspective, the meaning of life is having a mission that transcends the physical world. For example, to know and love God. Another would be attempting to tell eight billion people about a near-death experience (hmm, umm) so they can have a better idea of what faces them at the end of their days, and how to prepare for it.

IT MAKES NO SENSE TO HATE!

Hate will not get you the good afterlife. It cannot survive in Heaven. Take a tip from bizzaro world and "just (don't) do it". The people bound for Heaven WON'T hate. They will feel sorry for the hateful, knowing where the hateful will end up after "death", and they'll try to remedy the situation. Are YOU hateful? There is a fine place saved especially for you... you're going to HATE it! NAHHHH, don't thank us... you EARNED it!

IS THERE A LIMIT TO GOD'S FORGIVENESS?

While some argue that God's forgiveness is limitless and that He will forgive any transgression, no matter how heinous, others believe that certain behaviors may be unforgivable. What did the NDE have to say about it? It's somewhat obvious... if everything was forgivable, there would be no need for a "Judgement", or "The Void" (hell)... which has already been "shown" to exist. ...Something is not forgivable. Wouldn't rejecting God be one? NO, it is not limitless.

It is possible to argue that the limit to God's forgiveness is not so much a matter of God's own capacity to forgive but rather our own willingness to repent. If we continue to engage in harmful behaviors, refuse to acknowledge our mistakes, or fail to take responsibility for our actions, then it becomes increasingly difficult to receive forgiveness.

God's forgiveness is closely tied to the idea of repentance and redemption. In other words, brother, it is not enough to simply ask for forgiveness and continue to engage in similar behaviors. Instead, **true repentance requires a genuine effort to** change one's ways and **make amends for past wrongs**... I thought you ought to know.

HOW CAN WE MAKE AMENDS FOR PAST MISTAKES?

One should start by acknowledging the mistake because they're feeling genuine remorse. It's not enough to just say you're sorry without truly meaning it. Actions speak louder than words, so making an effort to make things right and restore what was lost or damaged can be a good way to show sincerity. This could mean offering an apology and making reparations then taking steps to prevent the mistake from happening again in the future. Doing nothing but saying you're sorry shows something too... and it's not good. The way you act now will show whether you're truly sorry or not, here and in the end.

HOW CAN WE BEST SERVE OTHERS?

With a side of broccoli? ...Just be willing to help, when and where you can. It's like money in the bank! It is truly a Heavenly bank account!

It is important to be compassionate. It helps us to feel the plight of others and respond with kindness. This may involve sacrificing our time, resources, and even our own needs at times to assist those who require our aid.

Be available and willing to help wherever and whenever possible. Doing so can make a huge impact on the lives of those around us, while we experience joy from helping others. After you have helped someone, you feel... especially good. As a near-death experiencer, I must say... that feeling you get after helping someone is how goodness feels in Heaven, ALL THE "TIME". Naturally, in Heaven it is infinitely stronger for the same act. The point? THAT IS the feeling of pure goodness, and we can have a piece of it in THIS life... by helping.

WHY DO SOME PEOPLE SEEM TO HAVE MORE BLESSINGS THAN OTHERS?

What constitutes a "blessing"? Is a new car considered a blessing even with the additional costs and responsibilities? What a blessing is varies depending on one's perspective. Some believe that all things ultimately work for the good of those who love God. Some individuals view their mere survival or employment as a blessing. It's like gratitude… it's all a matter of how you look at it. No matter what is or is not considered a blessing, it's mostly just the luck of the draw as to whether you get some. Sometimes it's just about being at the right place at the right time. Occasionally it only seems like others get more. Maybe they got short-changed elsewhere in life and the "blessing" you see is just the "evener". …Blessings are random… like life.

WHY DO BAD THINGS HAPPEN TO GOOD PEOPLE?

Have you ever wondered why unfortunate events happen to good people? Some might say it's a test, but in reality, it's an opportunity to highlight who you truly are in tough situations. Is love part of your solution when facing problems or is it nowhere to be found? The truth is life doesn't come with a guarantee of a perfect balance between good and bad experiences. It's unpredictable and random, as I know all too well.

HOW CAN WE TRUST GOD'S PLAN WHEN THINGS ARE GOING WRONG??

It's inevitable that things won't always go as planned. How can we trust in God's plan? We simply have to adapt and go with the flow. This has been the case since the beginning of time, even for prehistoric humans. Those who are able to adjust to change ultimately succeed at living. If the changes end up killing us, we still WIN, assuming certain things.

What is the Effect of "Forever" Like?

…Try this. Pick one of the new songs you've heard that you really like a lot. Play it. Play it again, louder. Keep playing it until bedtime. When you get up in the morning, play it again. Then play it again until bedtime. Nah, just leave it on all night…from now on… until you die. Soon you can't stand it. …The HORROR! And that's a song you LIKED! The moral of the story? Forever is a LONG, LONG… …LONG, LONG time.

WHAT ABOUT A FEW, MOSTLY LITTLE LIES?

Lying is just plain dumb, when you think about it. During life, once liars are caught in a lie, who will believe them in the future? Why even talk to them? What they say will likely be another lie. In the afterlife, it's even worse than that.

Liars are buying themselves an eternity of being lied to. No biggy? Let's say you find yourself where liars go. You haven't had a drink of water for a "week". Some evil SOB says he'll be right back with a truckful of water. You wait. You anticipate. You wait some more. You call out. No one answers. You LOSE YOUR MIND and scream out for water... for EVER... and THAT was only one "payment" for one lie (out of how many?). Wasn't that fun? You thirsty?

That "little white lie" that is so popular... does NOT exist as far as the afterlife is concerned. Little lies, big lies, deception, it's all the same! Every lie is right up there with the biggest lie ever told. The problem comes with the WILLINGNESS to lie, not the "size" of the lie. The same goes for theft. Stealing a pack of gum versus stealing peoples' life savings... at the life review, the same!

Knowing, now, how short life is, it's clear that lying is totally pointless. Life will likely seem to have been only moments long, once it's over. I often call it "ten minutes" long. So, the question becomes, can you go ten minutes without lying? Why spend a SINGLE moment of life lying, when in TWO moments the truth will come out for all to see? Besides ...all that does is prove to God that you are a LIAR. Liars don't do so well in the next life. In a ten-minute life? Who would lie??

HOW CAN WE FIND TRUE HAPPINESS?

In this life? **By being assured** that **the upcoming "permanent" life isn't ruined** before we even get there **by something we did in this "practice" life.** That changes everything, in the practice life... THIS life.

Finding true happiness can involve things like spending time with loved ones, pursuing one's passions, helping others, setting and achieving meaningful goals, and maintaining a positive outlook on life. Of course, these things are all more easily done when you discover that your future happiness is assured!

HOW CAN WE LIVE A LIFE FREE FROM WORRY AND ANXIETY AND FIND PEACE IN A CHAOTIC WORLD?

Achieving a worry-free and peaceful life in a chaotic world is a challenging task. One approach that works for me is to keep in mind that life on earth is temporary, and there is an eternal life of happiness waiting for us in Heaven. Performing good deeds when feeling anxious can also help. The hope is, the evil powers that are messing with you will lay off you, so that you'll quit doing good deeds (done because of feeling bad).

...You feel good. You're winning... relax a bit... take your shoes off.

WHAT IS THE KEY TO A SUCCESSFUL MARRIAGE OR RELATIONSHIP?

Why would I ask Jesus this? To get (just) another opinion??

With almost 50 years under our belts, it's sure that there are several factors involved. A sense of humor. Attention to the others' needs. Willingness to ALWAYS do 50% of the house/car/yard/childcare work/yes, diaper-duty... without being forced to. Willingness to occasionally agree that YOU were the person in the wrong... when you WEREN'T. Being independently wealthy doesn't usually hurt, either. (Should this be in reverse order?)

HOW CAN WE DISCERN GOD'S WILL FOR OUR LIVES?

Ask.

WHAT IS THE BEST WAY TO SPREAD THE MESSAGE OF GOD'S LOVE?

There are many ways to spread the message of God's love, and the best way depends on the individual's talents and resources. Some common methods include sharing personal testimonies, volunteering in community service projects, participating in church events, and using social media to reach a wider audience. The most personal would perhaps be door-to-door.

People are often drawn to those who exude love, compassion, and kindness, and may be more willing to hear a message about God when it is accompanied by genuine acts of care and service.

It's also important to approach sharing the message with humility and respect for others' beliefs. Trying to force someone into accepting a particular belief system rarely leads to positive results and can actually push people away. Talk to them, not AT them and listen to others' viewpoints, sharing the message of love in a non-judgmental way. That's "all".

LIST OF UNKNOWNS
Why Did YOU See Jesus but Not One of the More "Deserving" Kids in Town?

That's a good question... to ask Jesus when YOU get there. It couldn't be as simple an answer as, because this kid asked to (WITH gusto!), right?

DO OUR PETS HAVE AN AFTERLIFE, AND CAN WE BE REUNITED WITH THEM?

There is no scientific evidence as to whether pets have an afterlife and whether we can be reunited with them. Some religions propose the idea that animals have souls and may have an afterlife. There are stories about pets crossing over into the afterlife and reuniting with their humans.

There were no animals seen during this NDE. It wouldn't surprise me at all if animals have souls. During those flying dreams, MANY times I'd be flying over a shallow, sunlit valley that was covered with waist high grass with scattered trees. It all felt like it was alive, as in sentient. A glow came off the blades of grass as they waved in the breeze as if to say hello. There were no animals seen there... so that's no help. If grass is sentient, animals likely have souls, eh?

Pet owners find comfort in the idea that our pets will be with us in the afterlife. The question of pets going to Heaven leads to other interesting questions. Would they still have an animals' body? Can they speak? ...It's all mind-to-mind... I bet they can.

DO WE MEET OUR LOVED ONES (WHO HAVE PASSED AWAY) IN THE AFTERLIFE?

Not all visitors to Heaven get inside... unless the "court" yard is considered inside. There was only one person I laid eyes on. It FELT like there was a multitude of people... all around... all the people that ever lived... but the little bit of... moments... not "time"... that I had were spent looking at who I was "talking" with. There wasn't any immediate family to talk to. So, it is unknown.

IS THERE A HIERARCHY OR SOCIAL ORDER IN THE AFTERLIFE?

Some religions do propose there being a social order in the afterlife, with different places assigned to souls based on their deeds or faith during their lifetime. For instance, Heaven and hell is often presented as a hierarchical system, where souls are judged and sorted into different levels of reward or punishment based on their actions on earth.

In my near-death experience, I saw no evidence of a social order, but I can't imagine that I would have a place even down the block from the least of the Saints.

CAN WE CHANGE OUR APPEARANCE OR FORM IN THE AFTERLIFE?

We will be fully functional, free from defect, otherwise we're just the same, just not made of matter anymore. Can we change? Unknown.

WHY DID JESUS ALLOW HIMSELF TO BE CRUCIFIED?

The belief among Christians is that he allowed himself to be crucified as an ultimate act of sacrifice for the sins of humanity. It is seen as a demonstration of his love for humanity and a way for people to be forgiven and "make up" with God. The crucifixion is considered a central event in Christian beliefs.

HOW CAN WE DISCERN RIGHT FROM WRONG?

This must mean... in someone who can't tell right from wrong on their own. ...Does it build up, or tear down someone? Does it go against the "natural" rules of society such as don't steal, don't purposely injure, and so on? If you're not sure, ask someone (senior!) you can trust.

Something I was told WAY back when... if what you're doing gives you a sense of power, it's not inspired of Heaven. If it helps build-up someone, it is of Heaven.

ONE KNEW HIM AT 30 YEARS OLD, ONE AT 70...WHICH WILL I SEE?

The Bible doesn't give us a specific answer to this question. Some believe that in Heaven, people are transformed, so they may not look the same as they did on Earth. Some believe that people will appear in their prime, while others believe that they will be without any physical signs of aging. In the end, what people will look like in Heaven is unknown and can only be guessed at.

From a near-death experience point of view... Jesus wasn't all beat up. He was plump, and beautiful... for a man. I didn't think to ask the King of Kings to show me His scars...

WHAT IS THE PURPOSE OF SUFFERING?

Psychologically? It makes us appreciate NOT suffering. If there was goodness involved in suffering, Heaven would be full of suffering!

WHAT IS THE ROLE OF FAITH IN OUR LIVES?

For many people, faith provides a sense of purpose and direction in life, as well as a source of comfort and strength in difficult times.

Unless you've had an NDE, the best you can do is have faith that there IS a higher power who cares about you. Once upon a time I was in the same situation. The difference between then and now, after the NDE, is like night and day. Yes, "blessed are they that do not see, yet believe".

HOW CAN WE CULTIVATE A LIFE OF GRATITUDE?

One way is to focus on the positive aspects of life and to recognize the blessings that one has gotten. This can include gratitude for material possessions, relationships, experiences, or opportunities.

Another way is being present in the moment. Being aware of your surroundings makes it easier to appreciate the beauty of life. This can include the simple pleasures in life, such as a beautiful sunset, or a good book.

Practicing generosity and kindness towards others can also foster a sense of gratitude. By giving to others, making a positive impact in their lives, a person can develop a deeper appreciation for the good in their own life.

Or you can just plain realize that, if you live in a house and eat regular meals, you've got more than MANY people in the world do. Start there. Better yet, do without. You'll get gratitude.

WHAT IS THE SIGNIFICANCE OF MIRACLES?

Miracles are events that are considered to be divine interventions that defy natural laws and cannot be explained through scientific means. Miracles are believed to be evidence of God's power in the world.

Miracles can serve as a sign of His favor or as a confirmation of faith, demonstrating the power and love of God and providing hope and inspiration to believers. The significance of miracles comes from their ability to provide evidence and to inspire faith.

HOW CAN WE OVERCOME ADDICTION AND TEMPTATION?

Seeking guidance from God and relying on His strength can help individuals resist temptation and find the motivation to overcome addiction. It often requires several approaches, including spiritual, psychological, and social support.

Support groups or guidance from a spiritual counselor can be an important part. Being part of a community that shares similar struggles can give people encouragement and help them stay on track while recovering.

Healthy habits, like regular exercise, proper nutrition, and adequate sleep, can help individuals manage stress and reduce the risk of relapse. Finding healthy outlets for emotions can be a good way to manage addictive behavior. Professional help can be very important. They can provide a person with the strategies they need, as well as a chance to address underlying issues.

HOW CAN WE HEAL FROM EMOTIONAL AND SPIRITUAL WOUNDS?

It requires patience and time, like George said.

Speaking with God can provide a sense of hope and purpose. Forgiveness is also a critical aspect of emotional healing. These practices can also help to find inner peace.

Counseling can provide individuals with the tools they need to help deal with their past traumas. A support group can be an important part of counseling while healing from emotional and spiritual wounds. Being part of a group that shares similar struggles can help people find a sense of comfort in belonging as well.

Exercise, healthy eating, and getting enough sleep are very important in the effort to help individuals manage stress and promote overall well-being. A personal plan can help lead to long-term recovery.

HOW CAN WE RECONCILE SCIENCE AND RELIGION?

Science and religion can be reconciled by realizing the nature of science and religion. Science has its limitations. It is limited to studying the physical and natural world, while religion, not subject to scientific proof or disproof, can give insight into the spiritual and moral.

Religious texts were written with historical and cultural contexts, and understanding this can help people reconcile apparent conflicts. Both scientists and religious leaders can help bridge the gap……

DO YOU SLEEP IN HEAVEN?

Sleep is often associated with temporary rest or death, while Heaven is viewed as a state of everlasting joy and peace. I wasn't there long enough to need sleep, so I can't say for sure one way or the other. If there's no sleep, forever could turn out to be a very long time.

IS THERE SEX IN HEAVEN?

The Bible is not clear on whether there is sex in Heaven or not. Some religious scholars believe that sex may not be relevant in Heaven, as the focus is on spiritual and emotional connection rather than propagation of the species. Others believe that if sex exists in Heaven, it would be in a holy form, without any of the negative aspects associated with human sexuality.

All I know is, I haven't seen or had sex in the next life. What I can say for sure is that... during the death experience, people felt like they were unisex. Think about that... So... is it the case where the person you're married to could be exactly the same person... only the opposite sex from now, except for random genetics?

The nature of existence in Heaven is a mystery. Most clergy say individuals should focus on living a virtuous life, reducing the need to speculate on the specifics of the afterlife. Boy do they.

DO WE EAT IN HEAVEN?

In the Bible, there are references to a heavenly banquet. Some religious traditions also believe in "spiritual food" or "food of the angels" that is consumed in the afterlife. As far as the near-death experience goes, I must have been too late for dinner, I think. I missed out on the foot washing too. What's that? Oh. That was my job?

WHO WOULD HAVE A BETTER UNDERSTANDING

People who died and returned from the afterlife is all we have to provide a firsthand account of what the next life is like. To know positively how things function in Heaven, a person would likely have to stay there, leaving them unable to tell us details. People have had a firsthand experience of the afterlife. There are near-death experiences. These experiences are generally glimpses of the afterlife, rather than complete descriptions. While these are often difficult to verify, the similarity of the reports provides evidence that there IS something to it. The afterlife is beyond human comprehension. That was my experience.

GET YE TO HEAVEN

Perhaps you're starting to wonder if getting into Heaven is even possible. The expectations seem impossibly high, and even those who have had a near-death experience can't say for sure where the line is drawn. It hardly seems that a father would kill a child for falling short of perfection, so why would God do the same?

But here's the thing: somebody is getting into Heaven. It's not impossible, and it doesn't have to be some elite group of saints who have never made a mistake. It can be you. It's up to you to strive for it and make it happen.

It's true that the bar is high, but that doesn't mean it's unattainable. Perfection isn't required, but effort is. You have to want it, and you have to work for it. It's a process, and it's not always easy, but it's WAY worth it.

So don't give up. Don't think that it's impossible or that you're not good enough. Keep trying, keep learning, and keep growing. Treat them how you want treated and you can end up getting ye into Heaven.

WASTED TIME

Many people have a knack for wasting time - whenever boredom strikes, they turn to the internet, games, or other distractions to while away the hours. According to near-death experiences, when we pass on, we will look back on our lives and realize that much of it was wasted. It's a harsh truth that seems unjust.

Let's consider a comparison between a lifetime and eternity. If we could do piecework for just ten minutes and be rewarded with a lifetime of getting paid according to the output of those ten minutes, we would undoubtedly work with all our might during those ten minutes. However, we're talking about a lifetime here, and not everyone can be a saint. What is expected of us in this life is to give our best effort. It's up to us to decide what that means.

This example will help drive home the point about wasted lifetimes.

Imagine you're twenty years old with a decent job, sufficient funds, and plenty of friends. Time passes by, and before you know it, ten years... WHOA, forty years have gone by. You're now approaching retirement with little to show for it, having lost your well-paying manufacturing job years ago and settling for something less. You're going through your old papers and receipts when you come across your old lottery tickets. You decide to check them all, just for fun, to see if you ever came close to winning. And then, you spot it - a winning ticket worth $500 million, and you missed it.

Your entire life was wasted, and it hits you hard. You could have been living a life of bliss from that very day! All that was required was to work for a comparatively short while (one lifetime) and you'd be tremendously overpaid, forever.

This scenario is akin to someone not being told about what was learned during a near-death experience while there was still time to make changes. It's a painful realization that you could have done things differently, but then it's too late.

THAT IS HELL.

The place known as the Good Place is nothing short of spectacular - a paradise where everything is perfect. In contrast, the other place, which some call hell, is devoid of any light or warmth. There's no love, no music, no drugs or alcohol, and no respite in sleep.

A human being's sanity is based on certain assumptions, one of which is the notion that we can control the course of our lives. What if we suddenly realize that we have no control over anything, not even our eternity? Such a realization would be enough to drive anyone mad, especially when coupled with the knowledge that we are alone and abandoned in a dark, desolate place. Every evil deed we ever committed would be visited upon us in unimaginable ways, all while we are cut off from anything good or hopeful. To make matters worse, time does not exist, and there is no escape, not even through death, because you're already dead. This, my friend, is hell - it's not a fiery inferno... most of the "time".

THE END

TITLES BY THIS AUTHOR ON AMAZON KINDLE:

"No Doubt, You Were Dead" is the story of the NDE with a focus instead on foresight and ESP, instead of questions and answers.

"Blood-Thirsty Eight Ball Until You Are Always the Winner". At one time, the author was almost unbeatable when playing eight ball. You will be asked to change much of your present approach to the game and you NEED to be able to follow instructions. Just so you know what to expect... once you do this, most people won't want to play you anymore. They don't like to hear, "Oh, RACKBOY!". This HAS TO BE the BEST book on shooting eight ball ANYWHERE!

"The Kid with a Thousand Questions"... this book. It's about a kid who is trying to find the "meaning" of life and is willing to do anything to get the answers to his many questions... anything, including writing a book. A near-death experience changed everything!

Books on the drawing board by this author: (titles may change):

"Kickin' Roulettes' Ass". This writer lost at roulette once. Once. In 1979…$20, coming back from two hundred down… but "had to" leave.

"Kickin' Craps' Ass". It's only Craps. What's the big deal?

"Kickin' the Racetracks' Ass". Formulated nearly forty years ago, this will get you into the race.

""Coin Flips and Number Tips, Kickin' Ass. Coin flips relate to Roulette? …And everything else??

....

In memory of Darren Pointer... one of the best humans to ever inhabit this planet.

 I believe he was taken prematurely by Mr. Rump during phase one of the Rump Roundup. Which **Mr. Rump**? D.T. Rump, of course!

....

Made in the USA
Columbia, SC
07 June 2023